DEFINING DECISIONS

JEREMI J. SISCO

Copyright © 2025 by Jeremi Sisco

All rights reserved.

No part of this book may be reproduced, stored in a retrieval system, or transmitted in any form or by any means—electronic, mechanical, photocopying, recording, or otherwise—without prior written permission from the author, except for brief quotations used in critical articles or reviews.

For permissions or inquiries, contact:

Jeremi Sisco

Alliniskey (Instagram)

Alliniskey.com

Alliniskey@gmail.com

Printed in the United States of America

First Edition

ISBN: 979-8-218-65721-5

Cover Photography by Roland Saun

Interior design by Jeremi Sisco

Scripture quotations are taken from the **New International Version® (NIV)** and the **New King James Version® (NKJV)** of the Bible. Used by permission. All rights reserved.

Dedication

This book is dedicated to the young man who walked home from football practice, telling himself that nobody cared about his problems.

Young man, you were wrong.

Table of Contents

Preface	1
Acknowledgments	3
Introduction	5
1. Somebody Help Us	7
2. Sometimes You Have to Quit	15
3. I Went Back	23
4. Friends	31
5. Uncomfortable Decisions	39
6. Saying Yes to God	47
7. The Decision That Changed Everything	57
Key Takeaways	65
Conclusion	69
A Prayer for You	71

Preface

There's a moment in everyone's life where we come face-to-face with a decision that changes everything. Maybe you don't see it right away. Maybe it comes quietly, in a whisper, or maybe it hits you like a ton of bricks. But one thing I've learned is that the decisions we make—both big and small—define the direction of our lives. That's what this book is all about.

I didn't write this as someone who has it all figured out. I wrote this as someone who's lived it—who's wrestled with the consequences of bad decisions, stumbled my way through uncomfortable ones, and found redemption in the best one I ever made: saying yes to Jesus.

For most of my life, I believed football was my purpose. It was my escape, my identity, my hope. But when football failed me, I was forced to face the one thing I had been running from—me. And in the silence, in the brokenness, in the confusion, I found clarity. I found healing. I found Jesus.

This book is a collection of stories—raw, real, and unfiltered—about the journey of decision-making. You'll walk with me through the pain of quitting something I once loved, the fear of going back to something I thought I needed, the struggle of facing the unknown, and the joy of choosing a better path. And throughout it all, you'll see how God's hand was guiding me, even when I didn't realize it.

My prayer is that as you read, you'll begin to look at your own life with new eyes. That you'll reflect on the decisions that brought you here. That you'll find hope in knowing that no matter how far you've gone or how many wrong turns you've taken, one decision—just one—can change everything.

You don't have to have it all figured out. You don't have to know what's next. But if there's one thing I hope this book helps you realize, it's this: **God can use your story. Every part of it. Even the messy parts. Especially the messy parts.**

So, wherever you are, however you got here—I'm glad you picked up this book. Let's walk through this together. Let's talk about decisions.

And maybe, just maybe, you'll find the courage to say yes to the one that changes everything.

– Jeremi Sisco

Acknowledgments

I'm incredibly thankful for the kind of friends who push you to grow—the ones who see something in you before you even see it in yourself.

A special thank you to my good friend **Christopher Findley**. You lit the fire that started this journey. Your encouragement and example were a big inspiration behind me finally sitting down to write this book. I appreciate you more than you know.

But above all, I have to thank my wife, **Monique**.

You never let me speak negatively about my past. You reminded me that everything I went through had purpose—and that my story deserved to be told. You were the constant motivation behind this book. Thank you for believing that I was capable. Thank you for believing in me. Thank you for pushing me—both metaphorically and literally—until this vision became reality.

This book wouldn't exist without your love, your support, and your strength.

Jeremi J. Sisco

Thank you.

Introduction

This Book Is About You

Let me get this out of the way right now—this book isn't just about football. It's not about pain. It's not even about me.

This book is about **you**.

It's about the choices we make, the moments that shape us, and the honest truth that sometimes life doesn't go the way we planned. It's about that space between where you are and where you *want* to be.

Most of us are walking through life making decisions every day—some without even realizing it. But every now and then, we hit a fork in the road. And when that moment comes, it's not always easy to know what to do next.

That's what this book is here for.

I'm not writing this from the perspective of someone who has all the answers. I'm writing this as a man who's wrestled with hard decisions. I've had to walk away from dreams, face uncomfortable truths, and let go of what felt familiar—even when it hurt.

But I've also seen what happens when you make the right decision.

I've seen how God can take your worst moment and turn it into something beautiful.

I've seen how one decision can shift your entire future.

You might see parts of yourself in my story. You might laugh, you might cry, or you might just sit in silence with the weight of your own decisions. And that's okay. That's what this book is meant to do. It's meant to challenge you, to encourage you, and to help you realize that **your decisions matter.**

You don't have to be perfect.

You don't have to have it all figured out.

But if you're willing to take a step—just one step—this journey could lead you closer to the version of yourself you've been searching for.

So, take a deep breath.

Get ready to reflect.

Get ready to grow.

Because this isn't just another book.

This is a decision.

Let's make it count.

– Jeremi Sisco

Chapter 1

Somebody Help Us

"Call upon me in the day of trouble; I will deliver you, and you shall glorify me."
— Psalm 50:15 (ESV)

A Cry from the Heart

At an early age, under undesirable circumstances, I realized I needed help. I will never forget the moment I screamed for help at the top of my lungs.

My family had been moving around for years, but we finally found ourselves settled, living with a family member in a little town called Gainesville, Florida. I was still in grade school at the time. I remember that day clearly—just like any other, the school bell rang, and the teachers led us to our buses. I made sure to find my sister so we could sit together.

Every ride home, every ride to school, I made it a habit to memorize where I was. I don't know what prompted me to do it, but I always liked knowing where I was. One landmark stood out to me—a big white wall with a long-gated fence. That image was burned into my mind. "If I could just see that, I would know how to get home."

That day, like any other, we got on the bus and started our ride home. But for some reason, we couldn't remember our stop. The bus driver—God bless his heart—wanted to help, but he didn't know what to do. He just wanted to finish his route and go home. So, there we were—me, my sister, and the driver, the only ones left on the bus. And then, just like that, we got off. He didn't take us back to the school, but I can't blame him. I was the one who reassured him, saying, "It's all right. I know how to get home from here."

Because I had seen that big white wall and that long gated fence.

So, we started walking, up and down each block, looking for that familiar landmark. But I soon realized something terrifying—every street looked the same. Every street had a big white wall. Every street had a long-gated fence.

For at least two or three hours, my sister and I wandered, alone. And if I'm honest with you—I was freaking out. I wanted my sister to feel safe, so I played it cool for as long as I could. But I cracked. Fear overwhelmed me. The thought of being lost forever shook me to my core.

DEFINING DECISIONS

We were lost, and we had no idea where home was.

Making the Choice to Cry Out

I made a decision.

I screamed at the top of my lungs: "Somebody help us!" I yelled, I cried, I panicked. The last thing I wanted was to become one of those faces on a Walmart poster—the kids who never made it home. I didn't want people trying to remember what we were wearing or guessing what we might look like years later. I didn't want to be lost.

And that moment became a defining decision.

The decisions we make shape who we are. Every choice has an impact on our lives.

When I reflect on where I am today, I realize that I've defied the odds. A young Black man raised in poverty by a single mother. Never met my father. Earned a full-ride scholarship to the University of Florida to play football. It's a story we've heard too often, and it's unfortunate that it has to be that way. But my journey has been built on the decisions I've made.

Looking back at the moment I screamed for help, that decision was simple—I didn't want to be lost. I didn't want my sister to be lost. That principle has stuck with me throughout my life. I don't want to be lost. I need help.

Somebody help me. Somebody help us.

Admitting the Need for Help

One of the first things we must realize in life is that we need help. I know you've heard it before, but it's the truth. We need help. Some of us have been strong for so long, handling everything on our own. Others have been screaming for help, but only on the inside—too afraid to let the world hear it. But here's what you need to know: you have to let it go. You have to make a decision, and that decision can change your life forever. It's simple: ask for help.

Don't be shy. Don't be afraid. Don't worry about what other people may think. This is your decision. This is your opportunity to move forward. So, say it: Somebody help me.

The Power of a Response

Let me tell you what happened after I screamed that day.

A woman ran out of her house to meet us in the road. To this day, I wonder what she was doing before she heard a child's desperate screams. But she came running. And when she saw us crying, she took us to her front yard, where her husband was standing, ready to help. She tried to soothe us, pointing out her beautiful rose garden, while her husband prepared to take us back to the school.

Let me pause here. I want to praise God, because we were in a small town with only a few elementary schools. And by God's grace, this man knew exactly where to go. He got us back to the school, back into the arms of our mother.

But what would have happened if I had never opened my mouth and screamed?

Lessons from the Lost

I've carried this principle into my Christian journey. Too often, we try to do everything on our own. We forget who is actually helping us.

My walk with Christ has been an adventure—I'm sure many of us can say the same. That's just part of the journey of building a stronger bond with Jesus. You ask tough questions, you face difficult times, and through it all, you begin to see how He is working. But before any of that, the first step in our journey with Christ is realizing we need help.

I get it, some of us think we've got life figured out. We've told ourselves that we don't need anybody. We can do it all on our own.

I know, because I've been there.

I've taken those long walks home, convincing myself that no one cares about my problems. I've had people turn their backs on me. But I've also been stuck. I've been lost—physically and spiritually. And I've learned that it takes real maturity to be honest with yourself and admit that you need help.

Listen, I thought I knew how to get home. I saw the landmark—the white wall, the long-gated fence. I thought that was enough. But there were so many things I didn't take into consideration. So many things I didn't pay attention to. So many things I didn't have in focus.

I needed help.

And the truth is, my need for help started long before I ever got lost.

Spiritual Landmarks

Making the decision to ask Jesus for help was the best thing I have ever done in my life. That's why I'm here. That's why I'm writing this book. Because I know that the decisions we make that bring us closer to Jesus are the best decisions we can ever make.

I'm writing this book so that you, too, can share your testimony. So that you can tell someone about your encounter with Jesus, starting with the simple but life-changing decision to ask Him for help.

And listen—we cannot be shy when we ask Jesus for help. We have to scream it. Scream it like I did in the middle of that street. Scream it from the rooftops: Somebody help me!

Because the moment you do, God will come running to you. The moment you ask, you open the door for Him to start working in your life.

But it all starts with a decision.

A decision to ask for help.

Final Thought

There's power in the decision to ask for help. It may seem small—it may even feel weak—but it is actually one of the strongest things you can do. Whether you're walking the streets of a neighborhood trying to find your way home, or walking through the struggles of life trying to find peace, don't wait too long to call out. Help is closer than you think. God is not distant—He's listening, and He's ready. All He's waiting for is your invitation. So don't hold back. In the words of Kevin Hart "Say it with your chest." Somebody help me.

Reflection Questions

1. What areas of your life have you tried to handle alone, and how might asking for help change your situation?

2. What fears or doubts keep you from asking for help, whether from God or from others?

3. Think about a time when you finally asked for help. What was the outcome, and how did it shape your understanding of relying on others and on God?

Chapter 2

Sometimes You Have to Quit

"For I know the plans I have for you," declares the Lord, "plans to prosper you and not to harm you, plans to give you hope and a future."
— Jeremiah 29:11 (NIV)

A Question That Made Me Pause

I remember running into a college coach who used to train me at the University of Florida in the strength and conditioning department. He asked me a question: "Do you regret walking away from football? Do you regret quitting the team?"

I hesitated. Not because I didn't know the answer, but because I knew what he was really asking. There are things in life we convince ourselves we're meant to do forever. Growing up, I was certain I was destined to be an NFL football player—no Plan B. I was all in. My hard work paid off, and I earned a full-ride scholarship to play outside linebacker at the University of Florida.

That dream? It consumed me.

It wasn't just about football. It was about proving something. Proving that I could rise above where I came from. Proving that I was somebody. I didn't want to just succeed—I wanted to survive. I wanted to make it out. And for a long time, I believed that football was my only way out.

The Truth About Quitting

I know what I'm about to say may go against everything we've been taught, but I need you to hear me: Sometimes, you have to quit.

Understanding when to quit is one of the hardest and most important decisions you'll ever make. No one wants to be labeled a quitter. We stay in bad situations because we're afraid of what others will think. We don't want people whispering behind our backs, assuming we gave up when things got tough. I get it—I've been there. But hear me out.

From the age of 10 to 26, football was my life. It kept me out of trouble. Isn't that why most parents put their kids in sports? To keep them from making bad decisions? I lived and breathed the game. I spent countless nights watching Ray Lewis highlight reels on YouTube, dreaming of greatness.

Football was my outlet. I used to say, "Football saved my life." Without it, I don't know where I would have ended up. I poured everything into it. I sacrificed relationships, time, and energy. Nothing else mattered. If you got in my way, you were just collateral damage.

When Passion Turns Into Pain

But something happened.

One of the biggest decisions of my life hit me in the middle of a practice. If I'm being transparent, I struggled with my love for the game. It's never easy when you have people yelling at you, expecting you to perform at a high level when something inside you is missing. I fought through the pressure, but deep down, I was breaking.

Have you ever poured your heart into something, given it everything, only to realize it's destroying you? Have you ever loved something so much that when it lets you down, it feels like your whole world is crumbling?

That was me.

Football had become the very thing breaking my heart, and I didn't know how to handle it. The sport that had saved my life was now crushing me. And that day, in the middle of practice, it all hit me at once. I dropped to one knee and began to cry because I knew—it was time to quit.

Choosing Yourself

Deciding when to quit can save your life. At some point, you have to choose yourself.

Some things don't require our commitment when there's no positive return. Yet, we hold on to shattered dreams because we've invested so much. We keep pushing forward because we don't want to be seen as weak. But quitting isn't about giving up when things get hard—it's about recognizing when something is taking more from you than it's giving. It's about survival.

Football consumed my life. It strained my relationships with my family. I barely spoke to my brothers or my sister. I only talked to my mom every once in a while. Football had taken my identity. It had taken everything. And when I finally walked away, I didn't even know who I was anymore.

I hit rock bottom.

Alone in my apartment, a bottle of liquor in one hand and a weapon in the other, I was ready to end it all. Football had taken everything from me, and I didn't see a way forward.

Nobody wants to share stories like these. Nobody wants to talk about their lowest moments. But I have to tell you—sometimes, you have to know when to quit.

When God Steps In

Quitting left me at rock bottom, but that was the perfect place for God to step in.

Sometimes, we have to be stripped of everything just to hear Him. Sometimes, we have to lose everything to realize He is enough. Quitting isn't failure—it's an open door to what God has always called you to be.

You are not just one talent. You are not a one-trick pony. You are full of potential. But as long as you hold on to something God is calling you to leave behind, you'll never see it.

People's opinions don't define you. A 90-year-old man once told me, "What you think about me is none of my business." I want you to hold on to that. The fear of what others think should never stop you from making a decision that will save your life.

Sometimes, you have to quit because it's the only way to move forward.

Final Thought

Quitting isn't weakness. Quitting isn't failure. Quitting is sometimes the boldest, strongest, most faithful move you can make. If something is draining you, if something is stealing your peace, if something is taking more than it's giving—ask God if it's time to let it go. Trust me, what He has for you on the other side is worth it. You're not giving up. You're growing up. And that's what this journey is all about—growing in grace, growing in purpose, and growing closer to the One who knows the plans He has for you.

Reflection Questions:

1. Is there something in your life that you are holding onto out of fear of what others may think?

2. How do you differentiate between perseverance and knowing when it's time to walk away?

3. What is one area of your life where quitting might actually open the door for something greater?

DEFINING DECISIONS

Chapter 3

I Went Back

"As a dog returns to its vomit, so fools repeat their folly."
— Proverbs 26:11 (NIV)

Back to What Broke Me

I can't tell you that every decision I've ever made was a good one. Yes, I quit the team—but then I went back. I know, I know. But hear me out. It happens. Need I remind you; this book is about making decisions. And sometimes, we make the wrong ones. I made the decision to go back to playing football because, honestly, it was the only thing I knew.

Have you ever felt like that? Like your identity was so tied up in one thing that without it, you had no clue who you were? You couldn't see your other gifts. You couldn't see your other talents. All you could see was the thing you've always done. That was me. I had been a football player for so long, I didn't know how to be anything else.

I remember sitting down, staring at my hands, thinking, *I don't know how to do anything else with these.* I wasn't a carpenter. I wasn't an electrician. I wasn't a plumber. All I knew was football. So, with that thought, I went back to the game.

Comfort Isn't Always Safe

The decisions we make aren't always pretty, and sometimes they hurt us even more. I'm convinced that some of us return to bad habits simply because we've convinced ourselves that it's all we know how to do. We don't want to climb a new hill or take an unfamiliar path. And if I'm honest, that's what I learned about myself—I was scared of the unknown.

There's something tricky about comfort. Comfort isn't always safe. It's just familiar. And sometimes we settle for what's familiar, even when it's hurting us, just because we're afraid of what we don't know. We'll stay in pain just because we know how it feels. We'll keep doing the same thing just because it's predictable.

So, I went back. I returned to the very thing that had broken my heart. I convinced myself that maybe this time it would be different. Maybe I just hadn't tried hard enough. Maybe if I sacrificed a little more. Maybe it was the coaching staff. Maybe it was the environment. Maybe. Maybe. Maybe. But the truth is, my heart was no longer in the game. I was just afraid of letting go.

Mistakes Don't Disqualify You

That's what happens to us—we're afraid, so we make the decision that feels safest. But often, it turns out to be one of our biggest mistakes. I want you to know that it's okay to make mistakes along the journey. You will make mistakes. I haven't met a single person who has gone through life mistake-free.

Sometimes we convince ourselves that we need closure, but deep down, we're really just hoping for a different result. Closure can be tricky. It can disguise itself as healing, but really it's just us trying to make something broken work again.

That season of my life didn't last long. I suffered another knee injury—my third. Oh yeah, I forgot to mention, I had already undergone three knee surgeries—one ACL reconstruction and two meniscus tears. You would think I had learned my lesson. That would have been reason enough to walk away. But some of us are knuckleheads.

But even though I was hurting physically, emotionally I was drowning. I was frustrated that I was back in the same cycle. Frustrated that I had ignored the signs. Frustrated that I hadn't listened to what God was trying to tell me the first time. That's the dangerous part about comfort—it can make you deaf to wisdom and blind to warning signs.

God Uses Everything

But you know what's crazy? God has a way of taking our bad decisions and using them for something good. This time around, I started meeting players who were faithful Christians. Every so often, I'd find myself sitting in Bible studies, discussing scripture, and having deep conversations with people who were struggling with their own decisions. I started accepting invitations to speak to young high school athletes, sharing my story.

I didn't know anyone in this new place, yet here I was, being invited to give my testimony.

Sometimes, even in our bad decisions, we can find the light. God can use anything—even our mistakes—to steer us in the right direction. At the time, I didn't see it that way. I was just frustrated. My only concern was finding the doctor, starting rehab, and getting back to the field as soon as possible. Like I said, I was a knucklehead.

But looking back, I see that God was slowing me down. He physically stopped me from playing football so I could no longer run from Him. He used my third knee injury to set me on a new path.

A New Perspective

Here's what I know now: just because you went back to something, doesn't mean you have to stay there. Just because you made a mistake, doesn't mean you're stuck. God doesn't waste anything. Not your pain. Not your disappointment. Not your confusion.

He uses it.

God will take your setback and turn it into a setup. He'll take your mistake and turn it into ministry. That's what He did with me. He took a broken, frustrated, washed-up football player and gave him a message. Gave him a purpose. Gave him a new dream.

That's what grace looks like. Grace doesn't just forgive you—it reroutes you.

Letting Go So God Can Lead

The truth is, I didn't find myself again until I let go of who I thought I had to be. I let go of the version of Jeremi that I had built around football. And in that letting go, I gave God space to build something new. I started exploring ministry. I started reading the Bible more seriously. I started having conversations with people who were growing—not just grinding. And I realized I didn't miss football—I missed purpose. And purpose doesn't come from a profession. It comes from your connection to the One who created you.

That's why I'm writing this book. Not because I have it all figured out, but because I know what it's like to go back to something that was never meant for you and realize that grace was there the whole time, waiting to lead you forward.

Final Thought

So, hear me out—you WILL make bad decisions. You will convince yourself that a bad decision is a good one, and you will most likely suffer because of it. But even in that, God can use your mistake to open a new door. The question is—will you walk through it? Will you recognize that God is leading you somewhere new?

That's what this journey is about—making the decision to say YES to God and allowing Him to lead you in a direction that changes your life.

You went back? Okay. Now let God bring you forward.

Reflection Questions:

1. Have you ever found yourself returning to something you knew was hurting you? What convinced you to go back?

2. What fears have kept you from moving forward into the unknown?

3. How can you recognize when God is using a situation to redirect you toward His purpose?

Chapter 4

Friends

"He who walks with wise men will be wise, but the companion of fools will be destroyed."
— Proverbs 13:20 (NKJV)

The Power of Influence

We're going to talk about something that isn't new to you—something we hear all the time: **Choose your friends wisely.** A big part of making good decisions is choosing who we spend our time with and who we allow in our circle. Believe it or not, your friends influence you. Have you ever caught yourself copying something a friend says or does? Maybe it's a gesture, a phrase, or even a mindset. Next time you're around your friends, take a moment to recognize what you've picked up from them. The influence is real, and that's why we have to be careful about who we call a friend.

Now, I know finding good friends isn't easy. I'm not talking about just any acquaintance—co-workers, classmates, neighbors, or people you see in passing. I'm talking about **real** friends. The ones who have your back no matter what. The ones willing to grow and transition in life with you. The ones you can have deep, unfiltered conversations with. Those kinds of friendships can be rare.

For years, I searched for that kind of genuine relationship—a brotherhood. I've always been the friend who was more committed to the friendship than anyone else. I was always the one willing to do anything for the crew. Yes, I was a fighter, and trust me, you wanted me on your side. But when the roles flipped, I never felt like I got the same loyalty in return.

When Loyalty Feels One-Sided

Have you ever felt that way? Like you give so much to people who wouldn't do the same for you? Like they take your loyalty for granted? That's when you have to make the decision not to be a follower—to stop chasing groups that don't value you. Understand that you are different, and that's what separates you. **Own it. Accept it.** You have to be so comfortable with yourself that you're willing to go places alone rather than surround yourself with the wrong people.

For a long time, I was scared to do things by myself. The thought of sitting alone at a restaurant or event made me feel like I was being judged. But that's the wrong mindset. Some of us don't feel comfortable with who we are, and that's a problem. You have to be good with YOU—plain and simple. **Who are you?** What do you actually like? Not what your friends like. Not what's popular. **What do YOU like?**

So, I made a decision. I started going to restaurants alone. The first time was awkward—just sitting there, eating by myself. But eventually, I grew past that discomfort. I learned to enjoy my own company. I learned to like me. And when I got to that point, I realized something: **I didn't need to force myself into friendships that didn't align with who I was becoming.**

The Importance of Good Friendships

One of the best decisions I ever made was going to church. And let's be real—not every church is great at connecting with young people. That's just the truth. But when I found the right one, it changed everything. I walked into an environment that challenged me to grow. When I first got there, I didn't know Moses from Daniel. But I was hungry to learn.

I found a group of young men who were also searching for something deeper. There's something different about friends who want to grow. Some people are content staying where they are, stuck in the same cycles, making the same mistakes. But when you surround yourself with people who are hungry for purpose, direction, and a positive path, that energy becomes contagious.

So, we started searching for answers together. We weren't perfect, but we were open. We asked questions, studied scripture, and leaned on each other. That's the kind of friendship that matters. Friends who help you walk toward the life God has for you. Friends who don't just encourage your bad habits but push you toward something better. **That's what I found.**

Recognizing When It's Time to Let Go

Some friendships are seasonal, and that's okay. One of the hardest things to accept is that some people aren't meant to stay in your life forever. **People grow apart.** Sometimes, the friends you started with aren't the ones who will finish the journey with you. And that's not a bad thing—it just means you're growing.

I've had friendships that I thought would last forever, only to realize later that we were heading in different directions. And it wasn't even about drama—no argument, no fallout— just **distance** in mindset and purpose. **And that's fine.** If a friendship no longer helps you grow, it's okay to let it go.

Jesus had an inner circle. He had the twelve disciples, **not everyone can have the same level of access to you.** Some people are there for a season, and others are meant to walk with you long-term. **Be okay with that.**

Be the Friend You're Looking For

It's easy to focus on finding the right friends, but it's just as important to become the right kind of friend. Are you dependable? Are you encouraging? Do you show up when it matters? Being a good friend isn't just about hanging out and having fun—it's about building each other up, calling each other higher, and having each other's back when no one else does.

Sometimes, the right people will come into your life once you start becoming the kind of person who's ready for that level of connection. You attract what you reflect. So instead of chasing people who don't appreciate your value, start focusing on who you're becoming.

Make the Right Decision

Choosing friends is serious—it's not something to take lightly. If you don't have the right friends right now, don't stress. The ones you need are coming. And often, they'll be the ones you least expect. Some friendships will last a lifetime. Others will fade, and that's okay. What matters is that you surround yourself with people who uplift, challenge, and support you.

I've got a crew now. People I can call on when I need advice, accountability, or prayer. People who are choosing to make good decisions—not just for themselves, but for the people around them. And I've learned that the right friends make all the difference.

So, take your friendships seriously. **Be intentional.** And most importantly, **be willing to be alone rather than settle for the wrong company.**

Final Thought

I want to leave you with this: God cares about who's walking with you. He cares about the voices you're listening to, the advice you're taking, and the circles you're sitting in. Choosing your friends isn't just about popularity or comfort—it's about your purpose. The wrong crowd can delay you, distract you, or even destroy you. But the right people? They'll remind you of who you are and who God called you to be. Don't settle. Wait for the ones who will build with you, pray with you, grow with you, and fight for you. Because when you find them—it changes everything.

Reflection Questions

1. Have you ever felt pressured to fit into a group that didn't truly value you? How did it impact your decisions?

2. What are some qualities you believe are essential in a true friendship?

3. How can you become the kind of friend that encourages growth and positive decision-making in others?

Jeremi J. Sisco

Chapter 5

Uncomfortable Decision

"And we know that all things work together for good to those who love God, to those who are called according to His purpose."
— Romans 8:28 (NKJV)

The Weight of Difficult Choices

Let me be the first to tell you that sometimes you have to make uncomfortable decisions. And the reason they'll be uncomfortable is because they might force you to deal with something you never wanted to face. Sometimes making a decision unlocks an emotion that has been buried deep inside. We keep things trapped in a box, shielding ourselves from emotional hurt, believing that avoiding them is the best way to protect ourselves. But the truth is, these decisions are necessary for growth, even when they don't feel good in the moment.

For me, that decision was finding my father—whom I had never met. For 30 years of my life, I didn't know who my father was. I didn't know his name, never saw a picture, and had no idea what kind of man he was. The thought of bringing up this conversation with my mother terrified me as I got older.

Living Without Answers

You see, I grew up with a last name *(Powell)* that didn't belong to my biological father. I carried the name of the man my mom wished was my father—maybe it could have saved their relationship, but I never had that conversation to know for sure. I'll never forget the day I found out the truth. I was 12 years old, and my mother took me to the pool. I don't know what prompted her to say it that night, but while we were playing in the water, just the two of us, she suddenly turned serious. She looked at me and said, "Jeremi, I don't want you growing up thinking that this other guy is your father—because he's not."

At 12 years old, how do you process something like that? For the majority of my life up until that point, I had believed one thing, and in an instant, that belief was shattered. Not only was the man I thought was my father not my father, but I had never met him either. It was a shock, but even at that young age, I thought about trying to find him when I got older. Maybe the man whose name I carried could help me find my biological father. But I buried the thought away because, deep down, I wasn't ready to face it.

The Decision to Search

I share this with you because not every decision in life is going to be smooth. Some decisions will bring tears to your eyes. Yeah, fellas, that means you too. There will be moments that hit you so hard they make you pause. I don't know what that decision is for you—the one that makes your chest tighten or your stomach sink. But I do know this: on the other side of that decision is the truth. And sometimes, the truth hurts.

Many years later, my wife asked me a question that I had been too afraid to ask myself: "Do you want to find your father?" I didn't realize how scary that journey was going to be. I prepared myself for the worst, convincing myself that I wouldn't be disappointed because my expectations were low. And then, one day, the phone call came. My wife—who had done all the work in searching for him—finally called and said, "I found him."

Facing the Fear

I was scared. I was nervous. I didn't know how to process what she had just told me. I didn't even know what I said in response—she did all the talking. She gave me his phone number and told me, "He's waiting for your call."

We hung up, and I sat in my truck for three hours in silence.

We had already come this far. The decision had been made to take this journey. But the next decision was even bigger—was I going to call?

That's when I learned a valuable lesson: you have to fight through the emotions. Make the decision that helps you move forward in life. Make the decision that helps you grow. Sometimes it's going to hurt, sometimes it's going to be uncomfortable, sometimes it's going to be scary. And yeah, sometimes it's not going to feel good. But that's ok—because this is about changing your life for the better. If it were easy, everyone would do it. But some people are too scared. I always tell myself that I do the hard things in life because I'm built different. You are built different.

Lessons from Uncomfortable Decisions

Before I made that phone call, one thought kept circling in my mind: "I hope he likes me." That was my biggest fear. I hope he likes me. When we finally spoke, we talked for hours day after day. This story isn't just about me. It's about you, too. Maybe your uncomfortable decision isn't about finding a lost family member. Maybe it's about stepping out of your comfort zone, addressing a toxic relationship, or confronting a past hurt you've buried. Whatever it is, I want you to know that you have the strength to face it.

Every difficult decision you make has the potential to transform your life. It may not happen overnight, and it may not always go the way you expect, but the growth that comes from stepping into the discomfort is worth it.

Trusting God with the Process

What I didn't realize in the moment—sitting in that truck for three hours, scared out of my mind—was that God had been orchestrating this entire process behind the scenes. He knew exactly when I would be ready. He knew I needed healing. He knew I needed wholeness. Romans 8:28 tells us, "All things work together for good." Not some things—all things. Even the uncomfortable ones.

God didn't just bring my father into my life so I could know a name. He brought him into my life so I could understand my identity in a new way. He showed me that even the broken pieces of my story could be put back together for something beautiful. And now, not only do I have a relationship with my dad, but my children have a grandfather they adore. A missing link in our family has been restored.

It Was Bigger Than Me

Here's what I realized—my decision to step into something uncomfortable wasn't just about me. It was about legacy. It was about breaking generational chains. It was about giving my kids something I never had. Sometimes the hardest decisions we make are the ones that bless those coming after us.

So if you're facing something hard right now—if there's a conversation you've been avoiding, a truth you've been scared to uncover, or a person you've been hesitant to reach out to—I want to encourage you. Be bold. Step into the hard thing. Your healing, your freedom, and maybe even your family's future might depend on it. Growth is uncomfortable. It requires stretching, bending, and sometimes even breaking. But it always produces something greater. Don't shy away from the growing pains. Lean into them. Trust that God is shaping you into the person He created you to be.

You will never regret doing the hard work. You will never regret choosing growth. You will never regret making a decision that pulls you closer to purpose. I'm living proof of that.

Final Thought

Growth doesn't happen in comfort zones. Change doesn't come from staying in safe places. If you want to see God move in your life in ways you never imagined, you're going to have to make some uncomfortable decisions. And when you do, He'll meet you there—in the fear, in the uncertainty, in the silence—and He will remind you that He's always been working for your good. So, don't run from the discomfort. Lean in. Because on the other side of that uncomfortable decision is healing, growth, and a testimony that might change someone else's life too.

Reflection Questions

1. Have you ever avoided making a difficult decision because of the emotions it might bring up? What was holding you back?

2. How do you think facing uncomfortable truths can help you grow and move forward in life?

3. What steps can you take to confront a fear or unresolved issue in your life, even if it feels uncomfortable?

Chapter 6

Saying Yes to God

"Then Jesus said to his disciples, 'Whoever wants to be my disciple must deny themselves and take up their cross and follow me. For whoever wants to save their life will lose it, but whoever loses their life for me will find it.'"
— Matthew 16:24-25 (NIV)

The Power of One Decision

There are some decisions that will change your life forever, but I've realized that those decisions are often the hardest to make. They shake up everything we've ever known and force us to step into the unknown. It's terrifying. It's thrilling. It's life-altering. And yet, some decisions are worth the risk of hitting the reset button on our lives.

Can you imagine what it would be like to reset everything? To erase every bad decision, every regret, and every wrong turn? Kind of like when I play Madden and need to clinch a playoff spot—if I'm losing, I'll admit, I hit the reset button. I refuse to lose. Don't judge me.

But real life doesn't have a reset button. You don't get to undo your mistakes with the press of a button. What we do have is the ability to make choices that set us on a new path. The problem is, those choices are often the hardest to make. They require letting go of our past, trusting the unknown, and believing that what's ahead is better than what we're leaving behind.

And that's where faith comes in.

When Church Didn't Feel Relevant

I'm not sure when the last time you went to church was. Maybe you've grown up and started making your own decisions, deciding if you even want to go anymore. Maybe you were one of those kids who got dragged to church every week—like me—only to make church a thing of the past as soon as you had the freedom to choose. If that's your experience, I get it.

Church didn't always feel relevant to me either. It was just another routine: sit in the sanctuary, listen to the pastor preach, play with a few friends (if I had any), then wait for Sabbath to be over so I could enjoy the rest of my day. I remember looking at the clock, counting down the minutes like it was the last day of school. And I'm just being real—I knew all the songs. I knew all the Bible stories. But if I'm being honest, I didn't know Jesus for myself. I knew about Him, but I didn't know Him.

So, when I got older, I did what many of us do—I put church in the rearview mirror. I started making my own choices. I started chasing things I thought would bring me happiness, success, and fulfillment. But something was still missing.

Trying to Fill the Void

We try everything—hanging out with friends, going out on the weekends, chasing relationships, turning to drugs or alcohol, buying fancy cars, jewelry, clothing, or shoes. We collect all these things, hoping they will satisfy us. But they never do. We're still left with that empty feeling inside. And I know it sounds cliché, but trust me when I tell you—it's real.

That emptiness? That restless, unsettled feeling that nothing is ever enough? It's a God-sized hole that only He can fill.

That was my story. I had everything I thought I wanted. I had talent. I had opportunity. I was on my way to achieving the dream that so many chase. But none of it truly satisfied me. Something was missing. And even though I was working hard, locked in, focused, I still felt a void that training and accolades couldn't fix.

Jeremi J. Sisco

The Nudge I Couldn't Ignore

I'll never forget when I was training for my Pro Day. For those who don't know, Pro Day is when NFL scouts come to evaluate you, giving you a personal tryout to see if you're a good fit for their draft selections. I was getting some looks. I was putting in the work. Locked in, focused, and disciplined.

Every morning, seven days a week, at 5:30 AM, I drove past this little church—the church I grew up in. I passed it on my way to training and again on my way back. And then, one day, something hit me: "Go visit that church."

I ignored it at first. I brushed it off as a random thought. But the more I ignored it, the louder it got. "Go visit."

Eventually, I gave in.

So, one Sabbath morning, I pulled up in my car. I had all my jewelry on, tattoos showing, short-sleeve shirt—I wasn't trying to impress anyone. I already knew I'd be judged, so I figured I might as well be myself.

But when I walked in, I wasn't met with judgment. I was met with love.

People were happy to see me. They embraced me like I had just come home after years away. Which was true. One lady even said, "It's about time you came back." It was so unexpected. And in that moment, I felt something I hadn't felt in a long time: I belonged.

Not on the football field. Not in the endless pursuit of status, success, and material things. But here. In God's presence. And for the first time in a long time, my heart was full in a way that nothing else had ever been able to do.

The Decision That Changed Everything

That day, I made the decision to say yes to God. Some decisions will change the entire trajectory of our lives. This was one of them. And looking back, I realize that God had been calling me all along. He had been planting seeds, whispering in my ear, tugging on my heart. He had never left me, even when I had walked away.

But now, I was finally listening.

That's the thing about God—He doesn't force us. He gives us the choice. But when you say yes, when you surrender and truly let Him lead, your life will never be the same.

Faith Isn't a GPS

Some people think faith means having all the answers. That if you follow God, you'll know exactly where you're going, like punching an address into Google Maps.

But faith doesn't work like that.

Faith is stepping out, even when you don't know where the road leads. It's trusting that even when you can't see the full picture, God can. It's saying, "God, I don't know where You're taking me, but I trust You."

Faith is more like walking with your eyes closed, holding the hand of someone you trust. You don't see what's in front of you, but you keep walking because you trust the one leading you.

And that trust, that decision to say yes, changed my life forever.

What About You?

Maybe you've been feeling that nudge. Maybe you've been running. Maybe you're standing at a crossroads, wondering if it's time to stop chasing things that don't satisfy and start seeking the One who does. I can't make the decision for you. But I can tell you this: Saying yes to God is the best decision you will ever make.

You don't need to have it all together. You don't need to fix everything before you come to Him. Just come. Say yes. And watch how He transforms your life.

Are you ready to say yes? To take the leap? To trust God with your future? Because if you are, I can hear the Rocky theme song playing in the background, because you're getting ready for the fight of your life.

Let your faith lead you. Let that decision free you.

Final Thought

There comes a moment in everyone's life where you stop running, stop pretending, and stop hiding—and you simply surrender. That moment for me came when I said yes to God. It wasn't a perfect yes. It wasn't a yes without fear or questions. But it was real. And that real yes has led me to purpose, peace, and a life far beyond what I imagined. If you're standing on the edge of your own decision, I pray you take the leap. Say yes. God is waiting—and He has more in store for you than you could ever dream.

Reflection Questions

1. What's stopping you from saying "yes" to God right now?

2. Can you think of a time when God was nudging you toward something greater?

3. How would your life be different if you fully trusted God with your future today?

DEFINING DECISIONS

Chapter 7

The Decision That Changed Everything

"Forget the former things; do not dwell on the past. See, I am doing a new thing! Now it springs up; do you not perceive it?"
— Isaiah 43:18-19 (NIV)

The Power of a Single Decision

At this point, we have explored how our decisions define our lives. By now, you should understand just how valuable your decisions are and how decisive you need to be in making them. The decisions you make alter the course of your life, but it only takes one good decision to change everything.

We make countless choices daily—what to eat, what to wear, what tasks to prioritize—but you will always remember the decision that changed the game. It could have been the decision to choose the right girl or guy. It could have been the decision to take a chance on yourself and apply for that job you always wanted. Maybe it was a decision to go back to school, to walk away from a toxic situation, or to buy yourself something nice because you rarely do. Maybe it was the decision to have children or to change your lifestyle completely. Whatever it was, you remember the one that changed everything and if you haven't made that decision yet, trust me—it's coming.

The Day I Chose Jesus

The decision to follow Jesus and pour my everything into my relationship with Him is something I will never forget. I made that decision when I was at rock bottom, feeling empty and lost, searching for something more. You know that feeling? That void that nothing seems to fill? That deep, aching emptiness that keeps you up at night? That was me. I had tried filling it with success. With relationships. With ambition. With the dreams I thought would bring me happiness. But nothing worked. Nothing satisfied me. Until one day, I made a decision. It changed everything because when I chose to walk away from football, go back to church, commit my life to Jesus through baptism, and get involved in ministry, I thought I had lost everything. Football was supposed to be my game-changer, my ticket to success. But God had other plans. It's funny how life works—how one decision to get closer to Jesus can completely flip the script. And I have never been as happy as I am now.

All the years I spent playing football never brought me the peace and stability that Jesus did. He led me to an incredible wife. He taught me how to treat a good woman. He taught me how to treat myself. He taught me how to love others. And all of this came from just one decision: saying yes to Him.

When the Impossible Became Reality

As I told you before, I have the all too familiar African American story—the kid who didn't know his father, grew up in a single-parent household, and was raised in poverty. My athletic ability gave me a way out. I got to play for the University of Florida, a Power 5 school. I thought that was my big break. But let me tell you something: there are some things we believe are impossible, but when you trust Jesus, you realize that nothing is impossible.

I had grown up with a missing piece in my heart—a father I never knew. I carried the name of a man who wasn't my father, someone with no connection to my identity. I had never spoken his name, never seen his face, never heard his voice. The question of who he was lingered like an unanswered prayer.

When I made the decision to follow Jesus, He led me to a woman who would change everything—my wife. As I said in the pervious chapter, she looked at me and asked a simple yet life-changing question: "Do you want to find your father?" The timing, the courage, the faith—it all felt divine.

I was hesitant. How do you search for someone when you don't even know where to begin? But God knew. My wife began to look. Within two days, she found him. She turned into a full-fledged detective. I have to say I've never seen her in that mode before, but I guess those are the things you're willing to do for those you love. And just like that, I found myself in the driveway of a stranger—my father.

When we met, there was no awkward silence, no confusion. It was like our hearts knew each other. We embraced like we had known one another our entire lives. That's what God can do. He doesn't just restore broken pieces—He writes new endings.

Now my children, who once might've grown up asking questions about their grandfather, now know him. They know where they come from. And the gap in my family tree has been filled—not just with history, but with healing.

Living Out the Yes

If you take anything from this book, I want it to be this: Your decisions define your life, but the decision that changes everything is your decision to follow Jesus. Read His Word. Get to know Him. Pray. Be open. Let Him work in your life.

I promise you—it will be a game-changer. I know this journey isn't always easy, sometimes, saying yes to God is scary, trusting that He has a plan even when we don't see it. But let me tell you: there is no better decision you can make with your life than choosing Jesus.

Everything else in life is temporary. The highs, the successes, the material things—they all fade. But choosing Jesus? That's a decision that transforms you forever.

The Ripple Effect of Saying Yes

Here's what I've learned, when you make a bold decision for Christ, it doesn't just impact you—it impacts everyone around you. Your family will feel it. Your friends will notice the change. Your children will inherit a different kind of legacy. Because choosing Jesus doesn't just change one part of your life; it redefines your entire existence. And that's the beauty of it—when you say yes to God, you're saying yes to a life you could never have built on your own. You're saying yes to purpose. To healing. To restoration. To a legacy that lasts beyond your years. And maybe that's what God has been waiting for—your yes.

Final Thought:

This isn't just about me. It's about you. It's about your moment. Your decision. The one you know you've been avoiding. The one you keep putting off. That leap of faith you've been scared to take. Don't wait until rock bottom to decide to live differently. You don't have to hit your lowest to know God is calling you higher. Say yes now. Say yes today. Don't worry about how much you don't know, how far you've strayed, or how broken you feel. God can handle all of that. He just wants your yes. And trust me—once you give it, everything changes.

Reflection Questions

1. What is holding you back from making the decision to fully trust God with your life?

2. How has God already shown you that nothing is impossible with Him?

3. If you said "yes" to God today, what do you think would change in your life?

DEFINING DECISIONS

Key Takeaways

Throughout this book, we've taken a journey through decisions—some difficult, some life-changing, and some that came with a whole lot of pain and learning. But here's the truth that's been woven into every chapter: **your decisions define your life**. And sometimes, **all it takes is one decision to change everything.**

These are the key principles that have shaped my journey—and I believe they can shape yours too:

1. Ask for Help When You're Lost
It's not weakness to ask for help—it's strength. The decision to open your mouth and say, "Somebody help me," can change the course of your life. You don't have to walk through darkness alone.

2. Know When to Walk Away
Quitting isn't always a sign of failure. Sometimes, it's the smartest, most courageous thing you can do. When something is destroying you more than it's building you, it's okay to step away. Choosing yourself is not selfish—it's survival.

3. Own Your Mistakes and Learn From Them
We all go back sometimes. We revisit habits, relationships, or careers that once broke us. But God can still use those decisions to lead us somewhere new. Growth often starts in the place where you thought you failed.

4. Choose Friends Who Want to Grow With You
The people you surround yourself with will either pull you forward or drag you back. Be intentional about your circle. A real friend encourages your purpose, supports your growth, and walks with you through change.

5. Make the Uncomfortable Decisions
Growth requires discomfort. Whether it's confronting your past, forgiving someone, or facing your fears—those hard choices bring healing and freedom. Don't let comfort keep you bound. Break free.

6. Say Yes to God
The single greatest decision you can make is to say yes to Jesus. That "yes" might feel risky. It might feel uncertain. But I promise—it will change your life. Not just for a moment. Forever.

7. One Decision Can Change Everything
Whether it's reconnecting with a long-lost parent, walking away from a dream, or surrendering your life to Christ—**one**

decision can redefine your identity, your legacy, and your future. Don't underestimate what your next yes can unlock.

Final Thought

You don't have to have it all figured out. You just have to be willing to take that first step. God can do a lot with one decision. Especially when that decision is yours.

Conclusion

Well, there you have it.

Thank you for taking this journey with me—walking through some of the biggest decisions I've made in my life. My hope is that, along the way, you've had moments to pause. Moments to reflect. Moments where something in these pages connected to your own story.

Maybe you saw yourself in a few of the chapters. Maybe you thought about the decisions you've made—both the good ones and the ones that hurt. Maybe you even shed a few tears thinking about what could've been, what should've been, or what still could be.

But more than anything, I pray that this book challenged you to think seriously about the most important decision you will ever make—the decision to say **yes to God**.

That one decision? It changes everything.

It doesn't just adjust your direction—it redefines your destination. It doesn't just fix what's broken—it transforms you from the inside out. And it's the best decision you could ever make with your life.

So now, the ball's in your court.

What will you do with everything you've just read? What decision will you make going forward?

Will you keep trying to figure it all out on your own, or will you let the One who created you take the lead?

I want to close this book the same way I started it—with honesty, hope, and a heart that wants to see you win.

Let's pray together.

A Prayer for You

Heavenly Father,

Thank You for this reader. Thank You for bringing them to this moment—right here, right now. I pray that You guide every decision they make from this day forward. I pray they experience the peace that only You can give. I pray they say yes to You, wholeheartedly, without hesitation. Lord, show them the difference You can make in their life. Let them know that they are never alone, and that Your plans for them are good. Keep them, lead them, and love them. In Jesus' name, Amen.

www.ingramcontent.com/pod-product-compliance
Lightning Source LLC
Chambersburg PA
CBHW031256110426
42743CB00039B/594